ORCA FOOTPRINTS

Dig Deep

CONNECTING ARCHAEOLOGY, OCEANS AND US

NICOLE F. SMITH

ORCA BOOK PUBLISHERS

Published in Canada and the United States in 2023 by Orca Book Publishers.
orcabook.com

Library and Archives Canada Cataloguing in Publication
Title: Dig deep : connecting archaeology, oceans and us / Nicole F. Smith.
Names: Smith, Nicole F., author.
Series: Orca footprints.
Description: Series statement: Orca footprints | Includes bibliographical references and index.
Identifiers: Canadiana (print) 2022020697X | Canadiana (ebook) 20220206988 |
ISBN 9781459826083 (hardcover) | ISBN 9781459826090 (PDF) | ISBN 9781459826106 (EPUB)
Subjects: LCSH: Underwater archaeology—Juvenile literature.
Classification: LCC CC77.U5 S65 2023 | DDC j930.1028/04—dc23

Library of Congress Control Number: 2022935256

Summary: This nonfiction book introduces middle-grade readers to marine archaeology. Illustrated with photographs throughout, in this book young people will discover how understanding our ancient ancestors' relationship with the ocean can help the planet today and in the future.

Orca Book Publishers is committed to reducing the consumption of nonrenewable resources in the production of our books. We make every effort to use materials that support a sustainable future.

Orca Book Publishers gratefully acknowledges the support for its publishing programs provided by the following agencies: the Government of Canada, the Canada Council for the Arts and the Province of British Columbia through the BC Arts Council and the Book Publishing Tax Credit.

Front cover images by EmilyNorton/Getty Images and Alexander Mackie
Back cover images by Nicole Smith
Design by Teresa Bubela
Layout by Dahlia Yuen
Edited by Kirstie Hudson

Printed and bound in South Korea.

26 25 24 23 • 1 2 3 4

For Mom, Dad, Iain, Flora and all my teachers past, present and future.

Archaeological excavation in a rock shelter.
ALEXANDER MACKIE

A projectile point made from volcanic stone.
NICOLE SMITH

Contents

CHAPTER ONE
WHAT WE LEAVE BEHIND

CHAPTER TWO
LOOKING FOR OCEAN CLUES

CHAPTER THREE
LEARNING FROM OUR ANCESTORS

CHAPTER FOUR
ARCHAEOLOGY OF THE FUTURE

Introduction

This is me getting my hands dirty at an archaeological site in Argentina.
JUDE ISABELLA

Have you ever found a seashell on land and wondered how it got there? Was it dropped by a bird, washed in by a wave, dragged on shore by an otter or placed there by a person? Did you know you can look for clues that might help you figure out who moved it from the beach? Animal droppings nearby might give you a hint. Paint, drilled holes or carvings on the shell might tell you a person played a role. While you look around you might ask yourself if the seashell has been on land for days, weeks, months or even thousands of years.

I'm an ***archaeologist***, so I ask myself questions like this a lot. I study the ways people lived in the past. I examine their tools, clothing, gardens, compost, campsites, houses, villages, towns and even their fortresses. I investigate their ***aquaculture***, forestry and fishing technologies. And yes, I even study their shells. Often I find objects from the ocean on land because people have been using resources from the sea for thousands and thousands of years.

SG̱ang Gwaay Llanagaay is an ancestral Haida village and UNESCO World Heritage site.
ALEXANDER MACKIE

Most of my work takes place along coastlines. In British Columbia, I work with First Nations communities to understand some of the ways their ancestors lived. While stories and details are unique to each place, one thing that ties all coastal communities together, no matter where in the world we live, is our connection to the sea. Our ancient ancestors used and honored the ocean and its creatures—from tiny fish eggs and clams to giant humpback whales. What people have used and left behind can give us important clues about how our oceans have changed or stayed the same over hundreds and thousands of years.

In this book we will explore many ways people have used the marine environment around the world over the last 164,000 years, and we will learn how this knowledge can be used to improve the health of our oceans today. We'll also consider what we can leave behind for the archaeologists of the future to find. What will they think of us? Let's dig deep!

Herring eggs on kelp, cedar or hemlock boughs are delicious! NICOLE SMITH

CHAPTER ONE

What We Leave Behind

Seashells make beautiful mobiles.
RAWPIXEL/GETTY IMAGES

SEEING THE SEA ON LAND

Where do you find examples of the ocean on land? If you live in a city, you probably buy fresh fish, crabs, clams or shrimp in the seafood department of your local grocery store. But have you ever had an opportunity to catch your own fish, collect mussels or dig your own clams? If so, there's a good chance you left the beach or ocean and took your catch back home to cook a tasty meal. And what did you do with the bones or the shells when you were done? Maybe you put them in a compost bin under your sink. Or maybe you turned your shells into jewelry, rattles or wind chimes. If you did any of these things, you would have been engaging in activities that are thousands of years old. It turns out that using shellfish for food and art are two of the oldest human uses for marine species that we know about.

Rocky reefs like this can be covered with seafood.
TINATIN1/GETTY IMAGES

SEAFOOD LOVERS FOR 6,500 GENERATIONS

Around the world, our ancestors have been using things from the sea for at least 164,000 years—that's more than 6,500 human generations, or 60 million days! At Pinnacle Point on the coast of South Africa, archaeologists uncovered about two dozen shells dating back to that time, including brown mussels, periwinkles, limpets, whelks, chitons and even a barnacle that could only have lived on a whale! This is the oldest example of humans eating shellfish that archaeologists have found so far. For the ancient humans of Pinnacle Point, finding shellfish would have been easy. They would have picked them off rocky reefs at low tide. But finding a whale barnacle would have been more difficult. People probably didn't hunt whales 164,000 years ago, so they likely discovered a beached whale while gathering shellfish.

Whales may carry hundreds of pounds of barnacles on their bodies. Humpback whales carry a specific type of barnacle called the Coronula diaderma.
INSET: IAIN MCKECHNIE
WHALE: DAVID A. LITMAN/SHUTTERSTOCK.COM

They recognized a treasure from the sea when they saw one and likely collected the whale blubber, meat and skin for food and other uses. At the same *archaeological site*, researchers also found stone tools and red ochre. Ochre is a reddish mineral used for painting symbols on skin or decorating places like cave walls.

WHAT MAKES US HUMAN?

The discovery of ochre at Pinnacle Point suggests that early peoples were drawing and painting, but we can't be entirely sure until we find more evidence. Shell beads are definite examples of early human art. At Blombos Cave, another South African site, archaeologists found that people were making marine snail shells into beads 75,000 years ago—a time when ice covered much of Canada and parts of Europe and Asia. Researchers found even older marine snail beads in Israel, dating to 100,000 years ago. Recently archaeologists in southeastern Spain discovered that our *hominin* cousins, the Neanderthals, were also making beads and paint containers with shells at least 115,000 years ago. Creating art could be one thing that makes modern humans (like us) different from earlier human species like *Australopithecus afarensis,* or Lucy's species, who lived around 3.5 million years ago.

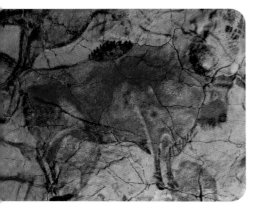

This cave art in Altamira, Spain, was painted using red ochre.
MUSEO DE ALTAMIRA Y D. RODRÍGUEZ/WIKIMEDIA COMMONS/CC BY-SA 3.0

These shell beads from South Africa are 75,000 years old.
FRANCESCO D'ERRICO, IMAGE COURTESY OF PROFESSOR CHRISTOPHER HENSHILWOOD

When you go clam digging, make sure there is no red tide in the area and that your catch is safe to eat.
LEFT: ANDREW GEIGER/GETTY IMAGES
RIGHT: TAK-PHOTO/SHUTTERSTOCK.COM

GONE FISHIN'

Our ancestors learned how to gather shellfish early in human history, but according to the archaeological evidence, it probably took them a while longer to learn how to fish. Fishing is harder than collecting or digging shellfish. Sometimes we can catch fish with our bare hands, but having a net, hook and line, or trap makes it easier. We can buy these tools or make our own fishing gear like many people around the world. The tools you need and the way you fish depend on the species you want to catch. You can catch many fish that swim near shore from a beach or a dock. All you need is a rod with a hook, some bait, a net and, most important, knowledge about what to do.

FISHING THROUGH THE AGES

Some of the oldest fish bones archaeologists have found are from easily caught fish that live near the shore. Some of the earliest fish bones come from Blombos Cave in South Africa. Here people were catching fish like the large black mussel-cracker and the South African mullet around 60,000 years ago! These nearshore species live in shallow waters near rocky shorelines. How people caught these fish back then is not clear. Archaeologists have found a couple of bone points here that possibly were used for fishing, but without more evidence

A hand-woven bamboo fish trap set up on a reef in Indonesia.
ETHAN DANIELS/SHUTTERSTOCK.COM

This bluefin-tuna bone was found at the Huu-ay-aht First Nations' 5,000-year-old village site of Huu$\underline{Z}$ii on western Vancouver Island. The bone is from the spine of the fish, where the tail begins.

A ground-shell fishhook from the Asitau Kuru rock shelter in East Timor.

we can't know for sure. We do know that people were using barbed bone points to spear fish as far back as 80,000 years ago. Archaeologists uncovered these points at a riverside site in the Democratic Republic of the Congo in central Africa, and they are the oldest fishing tools found so far.

SAILING THE SEAS

Finding the fishing gear that people used isn't easy. Wood, bone and shell—common materials for making fishing hooks and harpoons—decompose easily. This is also true of the roots, barks, kelps and other fibers that would have been used to make fishing lines and nets. After the barbed bone points in the Congo, the next-oldest fishing tool ever found is a ground-shell fishhook from the Asitau Kuru rock shelter in East Timor. People probably baited this hook to catch nearshore fish such as the triggerfish or snapper. Archaeologists think this **artifact** is between 23,000 and 16,000 years old.

Humans lived at Asitau Kuru for a long time. Archaeologists have recovered over 38,000 fish bones, some of which are 44,000 years old. Many of the bones come from nearshore species, but almost half of the bones are from such species as tuna, rays and sharks. These marine creatures live deep in the open ocean, coming to shore occasionally. Finding their bones on land provides us with *indirect evidence* that people may have had boats to travel offshore. They would also have needed sophisticated fishing gear to catch such swiftly moving fish. Researchers often argue about the meaning of indirect evidence, but it does seem likely that people had watercraft as early as 65,000 years ago. At that time people started moving to the areas known today as Australia and Papua New Guinea, but people couldn't have walked there! They had to travel by water because these places were separated from the Asian continent by about 55 miles (89 kilometers) of ocean.

COASTAL ARTIFACTS

Archaeologists call any object that you can pick up and move around, and that is made or shaped by people, an artifact. The bone harpoon points and shell fishhook, for example, were purposefully whittled and ground to give them their shape. These are artifacts and **direct evidence** of people's fishing gear and activities. There are thousands of different kinds of artifacts related to people's use of the sea. They range from clay octopus pots and eel-catching bamboo tubes to split timbers and metal rods joined together to make baskets and traps for fish and crustaceans such as shrimp and prawns.

Boats too provide direct evidence of humans' use of the sea—dugout canoes, bamboo rafts, reed boats, sealskin kayaks, birchbark canoes, moose-hide or reindeer-skin boats, sailboats, junks, motorboats and outriggers are all proof of people's maritime ingenuity. While many people anchored or moored their boats at sea, like we still do today, sometimes boats were pulled to shore for storage or repair. Sometimes we even find canoes in the rainforest!

Below is a partially finished canoe in the rainforest of Haida Gwaii. In the photo on the right, archaeologists are excavating next to a canoe blank.
BOTTOM: CHASE CLAUSEN/SHUTTERSTOCK.COM; RIGHT: IAIN MCKECHNIE

At this seaside village in Argentina, shells have been used as a landscaping material between the fence and the ditch.
NICOLE SMITH

WHAT'S MADE BY PEOPLE BUT CAN'T BE PICKED UP?

In addition to artifacts and faunal remains (the shells and animal bones that ancient peoples left behind), archaeological *features* contain information about the marine environment. Features are made by people, but they cannot be picked up or moved without being taken apart. Roads, sidewalks, campfire pits and rock walls are a few examples. Can you think of more? Roadbeds made out of crushed Japanese oyster shells are examples of features we see today that make use of an ocean resource. As we look back over thousands of years, we see that people used similar landscaping techniques on the Pacific coast of North America. Instead of using the introduced Japanese oyster, the ancestral First Nations and Native Americans used the shells of butter, littleneck and horse clams to create large, flat, dry areas where they could build their towns and villages.

A WHALE OF A TIME

Archaeological features can even be made from whales. Whales are some of the largest mammals on earth. They provide meat, and their bones, skins, sinew, blubber, teeth, ivory and baleen have been used to heat and light homes, make tools and even build houses. At the Ozette village on the Olympic Peninsula of Washington State, Makah ancestors used whale scapulae (shoulder blades) to line drainage trenches below their houses. Their Nuu-chah-nulth neighbors to the north used whale vertebrae and boulders to stabilize house posts as far back as 2,000 years ago.

It turns out we can learn a lot about the health of the ocean from the things people have left behind, lost or thrown away. In fact, we can examine their artifacts, faunal remains and features to figure out if our oceans are better or worse today than they were in the past. To do this, though, we have to think like detectives. We have to find the right evidence and then know how to study it.

This wooden house post from the ancestral Huu-ay-aht village of Ḵiix̣in is likely secured and held in place by whale bone and boulders underground.
NICOLE SMITH

Field Notes

Nuu-chah-nulth Nations along the west coast of Vancouver Island and the Makah People from the Olympic Peninsula have a long tradition of whaling. The first archaeological dig I ever worked on was at the Tseshaht First Nation's village of Ts'ishaa in the Broken Group Islands. By the end of the summer, the team had dug down 13 feet (4 meters) and found a feature built from whalebone, which included the skull of a humpback whale. Amazingly, embedded in the skull was the remnant of a harpoon blade made out of mussel shell!

This whalebone feature at Ts'ishaa (left) was four meters underground. On the right is a close-up of a mussel-shell harpoon blade that was found embedded in the whale skull.
LEFT: NICOLE SMITH
RIGHT: ALAN MCMILLAN AND DENIS ST. CLAIRE

CHAPTER TWO

Looking for Ocean Clues

ARCHAEOLOGICAL SITES ARE EVERYWHERE

A National Park Service archaeologist digs a test pit to look for archaeological materials below the modern concrete in the Fort Vancouver National Historic Site.
NPS PHOTO

I grew up on Vancouver Island, surrounded by what many people called "wilderness." The ancient places I learned about in school were in other parts of the world, like Egypt and Greece, where stone pyramids and buildings survived. So when I first started studying *archaeology* in university, I thought archaeological sites, especially where I grew up, were rare. Fortunately I quickly learned I was wrong. Millions of people have come before us, and they didn't always use stone to construct their buildings and towns. They often used materials that decompose. Over the years I've come to realize archaeological sites are everywhere—on mountaintops, on glaciers, deep in the forest and even underwater. Sometimes there are artifacts and features under the sidewalk you walk on every day! Humans tend to build on top of places where people have lived before, and this often means that evidence of the past can be right underfoot.

Can you imagine what a place would look like if the shoreline were higher? Or lower? Or if there were fewer trees?
DHARITRI WALIA / EYEEM/GETTY IMAGES

But how do we find an archaeological site? We start by imagining how our surroundings may have been different hundreds or thousands of years ago. We need to ask what a place would look like if we took away the houses, buildings and roads. And what would the area look like if the bodies of water were different? A section of river that is now straight may once have been curved. Or a dam on a river may have created a new lake where there used to be a forested valley. If you live near the ocean, it's possible that where you go to school, play soccer or visit your friends may once have been underwater. We have to imagine how the vegetation may have changed too. The forest where you climb trees may once have been a grassy plain.

Arti-fact

Sometimes you can find seashells in a lake. The shells are a clue that the sea level was once higher and the lake used to be ocean.

17

AT THE BOTTOM OF A BOG

One way archaeologists determine what an environment looked like in the past is to study samples of mud from the bottom of bogs, ponds, lakes or oceans. Yes, mud! We do this by pounding long plastic tubes, called core tubes, into the mud. We often have to do this while balancing carefully on canoes, rafts or boats. When we pound the tube down, it collects **sediment** from the bog bottom, lake bed or seafloor. Once the tube is full, we pull the "sediment core" back up to the boat using winches and pulleys. When we split open these tubes, we can see all the different layers of mud that have accumulated below the water over thousands of years.

The layers of sediment at the bottom of the core are the oldest, while the ones at the top are the most recent. Within the layers of mud we can look for evidence of how the environment may have changed. We can study the glass skeletons of small organisms called **diatoms**. These samples tell us if the water was salty or fresh. The pollen and seeds preserved in the layers of mud can show us what types of plants and trees grew there in the past.

(Left) These archaeologists are collecting a sediment core while standing on plywood that is lying across two canoes. (Right) Layers of sediment are revealed when the core tube is opened. (Inset) We need a microscope to see diatoms because they're so small!

LEFT AND RIGHT: ALEXANDER MACKIE
INSET: OXFORD SCIENTIFIC/GETTY IMAGES

When archaeologists find a place with high potential for containing evidence of people's activities in the past, we dig shovel test pits to look for charcoal, artifacts or features. If we find something, we then dig carefully with hand trowels and open up a larger excavation unit like the one pictured here.

ALEXANDER MACKIE

LOOKING FOR CLUES

Once we understand how the landscape has changed, we then have to look for places that would have been good for people to use. A hill may have been a lookout for hunting animals. A rock shelter or cave may have been a campsite. The shore of a protected bay may have been the site of a village. Once we've found a suitable place, we look for evidence of people's activities from the past. Just like us, our ancestors lost objects and left things behind. These discarded artifacts are the clues we use to imagine and reconstruct our ancestors' stories. One of the most long-lasting materials humans have used is stone. Archaeologists know a lot about how people made stone tools, carvings, walls and buildings. We also look for charcoal,

Arti-fact

If you find an artifact, don't collect it! Most countries have laws that protect archaeological sites. This means it can be illegal to dig or collect artifacts without a government permit and permission from the local Indigenous communities.

Limestone caves are stable natural cavities that are formed over thousands and even millions of years.
IAIN MCKECHNIE

which might show where people once built fires. And we know that in the right settings, animal bones and shells can be evidence of what people ate.

Any place where we discover physical evidence of people's past activities is an archaeological site. Sites can be big or small. They might be miles long and full of thousands of artifacts, buildings and roads, like the ancient city of Teotihuacan near Mexico City. Or they could be less than a square foot and consist of just one or two stone tools.

Any time we dig an excavation unit, we screen all the dirt to make sure we don't miss anything small. Here the team is screening shell midden and collecting all the fish, bird and mammal bones they can find.
NICOLE SMITH

HUMANS CAN CHANGE THE WORLD

Just as shorelines, rivers and plants have changed, animals have changed over time too. At the end of the last *glaciation*, there were many large mammals, such as the mastodon, mammoth, bison, short-faced bear, saber-toothed tiger and giant ground sloth, that no longer exist. For the better part of the past 5,000 years, the earth's environments, plants and animals were fairly similar to what we see today. However, in the most recent 400 years we humans have made big changes to how we live.

The **Industrial Revolution**, which began in the mid-1700s, substantially changed the way we live our lives. We harvested resources like trees and plants differently, and we used more of them. We mined for coal and drilled for oil to power our machines. The faster pace and more intense use of resources since then has caused our environments, plants and animals to change very quickly.

Today we are all affected by climate change. For the first time in the earth's history, people are the cause of rising sea levels, devastating forest fires and extreme weather. But by learning about what we have done in the past to create these changes, we can work to make things better again in the future.

Most woolly mammoths went extinct around 10,500 years ago, but a small population lived on Wrangel Island in the Arctic Ocean until 4,000 years ago.
DOTTED YETI/SHUTTERSTOCK.COM

MANY WAYS TO CATCH A FISH

For about 5,000 years prior to the Industrial Revolution, fishing technologies around the world were similar. *Jigging*, spearing, or using a fishing line with a single hook were common. People could catch more fish at one time by using baskets, nets, or wooden or stone-walled traps on rivers or along shorelines. However, the number of fish caught was limited by how quickly people could preserve the fish before they went bad. Many societies also had laws and rules about who could fish and how many fish could be caught at one time. In the 1800s new technologies allowed boats near cities and towns to collect many tons of fish.

People around the world use intertidal stone-walled fish traps. This one is from Tseshaht First Nation's territory in the Broken Group Islands on the west coast of Vancouver Island.
NICOLE SMITH

Instead of jigging, using lines with a single hook, or catching fish in traps, people used fleets of boats towing large nets to trap schooling fish. They also laid long lines with multiple hooks to catch bottomfish or used special vertical nets called gill nets to entangle fish. Even though people could catch more fish, they still had to be careful not to catch too many or the fish would spoil.

SALTING, SMOKING AND FREEZING

The main way of preserving fish in European and North American cities in the 1800s was to salt and dry them. Smoking was another common method of preserving fish. But if people caught too many, they couldn't dry them fast enough. The boats also could only hold a certain number of fish. In the late 1800s steam-powered ships were invented. They allowed people to travel out to sea and get home faster. As a result, fish populations quickly declined in areas close to shore. The faster fishing boats had to go even farther out to find the fish. In the 1920s, boats began to carry freezer systems on board. This new way of storing fish meant fishing boats could catch even more fish, and people didn't have to worry about the fish going bad.

SOMETHING FISHY'S GOING ON

While the new technologies were good for people and the economy, can you imagine what happened to the fish? Their populations declined. By the 1950s, scientists around the world had started collecting data on the number of fish in the oceans. By that time, however, there had already been many years of overfishing. This means we don't know the exact size of fish populations before modern fishing technologies came into use. But there are other places we can look for environmental information that go back hundreds and thousands of years. Can you guess what some of those are? If "archaeological sites" was one of your answers, you're right!

My very favorite way to eat fish is smoked.
JMP TRAVELER/GETTY IMAGES

Field Notes

I grew up along the shores of Nanoose Bay on Vancouver Island. This bay held one of the largest herring runs on the coast for thousands of years. In the 1970s, when I was a toddler, there would be so many fishing boats in the bay that my mom and dad said it looked as if there was a floating city on the water. Our neighbor, who was a fisherman, earned enough money in one night of herring fishing to buy his house. The bounty didn't last long though. After a few years there were very few herring left in the bay, and the flotilla of boats never returned.

FISH 'N' CHIPS, PLEASE

By studying archaeological sites, we can understand how plants and animals from hundreds and thousands of years ago may be similar to or different from today's. When archaeological sites contain faunal remains—the bird, mammal, fish or shellfish remains from people's previous meals—we can learn a lot about what animals were like in the past. If you've eaten fish and chips recently, there's a good chance you were eating cod. Cod has been an important fish on the east coast of North America for thousands of years. Archaeologists in the Gulf of Maine have studied cod bones in archaeological sites. By looking at the shape of bones, we can tell what fish people in the past were catching. We can also calculate how many fish they caught and how big they were. Archaeologists have found that Indigenous ancestors were catching much bigger cod than fishers catch today. In fact, the average cod between about 500 and 5,000 years ago was 3.3 feet (1 meter) long, while today it's a foot (30 centimeters). This is likely because of overfishing during the last 250 years, which focused on catching the biggest and oldest fish.

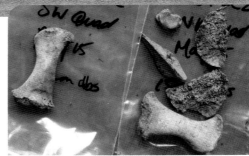

Top: Sea-mammal bones like these can be found in coastal archaeological sites.

Bottom: Chum salmon enter streams in the fall to spawn. During breeding, the male salmon's teeth change shape. When archaeologists find hooked salmon teeth in an archaeological site, they know that past Peoples caught male chum salmon in the fall, as that's the only time the teeth change.
NICOLE SMITH

23

Shellfish are full of healthy vitamins and minerals.
STEFANO EMBER/SHUTTERSTOCK.COM

Sea lions, fur seals and seals can be hard to tell apart, but if you look closely, sea lions and fur seals have small external ears that stick out from their heads, whereas seals have ear holes. Fur seals and sea lions are also really loud!

TONY BECK/500PX/GETTY IMAGES

YOU ARE WHAT YOU EAT!

We can also use archaeological data to understand how sea mammals' lives have changed in recent times. Have you ever heard the expression "you are what you eat"? Well, it's true! Our bodies absorb nutrients from the food we eat, and those nutrients help grow things like your hair, bones, fingernails and toenails. Scientists can analyze the chemistry of our hair or fingernails to learn if we've eaten meat, seafood or lots of vegetables over the last few months. In the case of sea mammals, which spend most of their lives in the ocean, their bones can tell us if they've lived in calm water or along rugged shorelines with strong wind and waves. Even sea-mammal teeth tell a story. As a fur seal gets older, its teeth get bigger. A new layer of tooth forms each year.

Whatever the fur seal eats in a year will leave a chemical signal in the new layer of tooth. This means scientists can figure out what a fur seal was eating during each year of its life.

ANIMAL BEHAVIOR CHANGES QUICKLY

In Argentina, archaeologists and ecologists compared the bones of fur seals today with fur-seal bones from archaeological sites to see how the animals' diet has changed. The research showed that in the past, fur seals ate foods found in protected inlets away from stormy seas. Today, however, fur seals grow up on the outer coast and around the exposed islands of Tierra del Fuego, at the southern tip of South America. Why would the fur seals go elsewhere? The scientists think it may have to do with overhunting and overfishing in recent times, which scared the fur seals away from their food sources in protected waters. Many sea mammals, including fur seals, came close to going extinct in Tierra del Fuego. Extinction was prevented when Argentina banned seal hunting in 1949. This example shows us how quickly animal behavior can change in response to people's actions, and that animals can pass their fear and knowledge of danger along to their babies.

OPENING OUR HEARTS, MINDS AND EARS

As you can see, even though we don't have written scientific data going back hundreds or thousands of years, we can be detectives and find useful information in other places, such as archaeological sites. And fortunately, in many parts of the world, there are people we can ask about how the oceans have changed over the centuries and *millennia*. By having open minds and listening carefully, we can learn from the Indigenous peoples whose families have often lived in the same place for hundreds and thousands of years. From them we can learn even more about how to manage and restore the health of our oceans for generations to come.

Arti-fact

People around the world have hunted pinnipeds—sea mammals with front and rear flippers, such as seals and sea lions—for thousands of years. The animals' bones and skins are excellent for making tools, boats and clothing. The thick blubber that insulates them from the cold can be made into a rich oil. And, of course, their meat is a nutritious food.

An archaeologist's job includes many activities. Dr. Maria Paz Martinoli usually studies fur-seal bones and teeth, but here she's screening dirt, looking for stone tools at a 5,000-year-old site in Argentina.
NICOLE SMITH

CHAPTER THREE

Learning from Our Ancestors

HAPPY CLAMS

These littleneck and butter clams taste great steamed, fried or smoked.
NICOLE SMITH

Have you ever walked out on a sandy beach at low tide and been squirted by a clam? Or jumped next to a *geoduck* hole in hopes you might get your parents or friend wet? If not, I highly recommend it. This was one of my favorite activities as a kid. I also loved digging for manila clams with my mom and steaming them at home to eat with melted garlic butter. Every time we dug, we learned that clams dig too, except they do it with their feet. We discovered that some are faster than others, some live near the beach surface and others like to bury themselves a foot down. We found out clams can close up fast, and you don't want to get your finger caught! When we brought our clams home, we had to put them in a bucket of salt water for a day so they could spit out the sand inside them, or we'd get a crunchy surprise when we ate them. My mom didn't dig for clams when she was growing up, so we learned what to do together. Imagine how much more we would have known if my mother had learned from her mother and her grandmother. We would have had the benefit of generations of knowledge about clams and the ocean.

You have to practice a lot to become a good spear fisher!
SUZANNE LONG/ALAMY STOCK PHOTO

FISHING IN THE TORRES STRAIT ISLANDS

In the eastern Torres Strait Islands between Australia and Papua New Guinea, Meriam people eat a lot of seafood. Their ancestors began living on these islands at least 2,800 years ago. Today everyone, even the kids, is involved in fishing and gathering seafood. Meriam children receive their first fishing spear, made from bamboo with iron prongs at one end, when they are toddlers. Children carry these spears with them whenever they visit the beach and keep an eye out for small sardines along the shore. By age four the children may join a parent to gather shellfish on the flat reefs at low tide. They quickly learn which shellfish are good to eat and which are dangerous. They also learn how to spot large marine snails camouflaged against the sand and broken pieces of coral. They see how their parents break and discard the shell and save the meat. By age six the children are allowed to gather shellfish with their friends. While having fun, the younger children continue to learn from the older ones.

HOW DO FISH BEHAVE?

As their experience and knowledge of the beaches grow, Meriam children begin fishing with a handline. To be successful they have to understand the tides, water currents and how fish behave in different seasons and weather. They have to know what the different species of fish like to eat. A piscivorous fish (a fish that eats other fish) will need different bait than an omnivorous fish (a fish that eats meat and plants) or a herbivorous fish (a fish that eats plants). To catch a piscivorous fish with a handline, the children have to catch live bait first. Once they've caught a small fish, they re-hook it quickly and then fling the fishing line out again to catch a larger fish. It's a complicated set of fast moves that takes practice to get right.

Similarly, spearfishing requires quick reflexes and good coordination and takes time to master. Even though most children receive a spear at a young age, they don't become skilled spear fishers until after age 10. By this time the children are no longer catching small sardines but have learned to find larger fish and squid in the lagoons at low tide. By their tweens, children know where to spear their prey by examining the ripples on the surface of the water. With a good eye, patience and practice, many children between the ages of 10 and 14 may become better spear fishers than their parents, especially if the adults don't practice!

Fishing with a handline from shore requires good coordination and knowledge of fish behavior.
PAULHARDING00/SHUTTERSTOCK.COM

The Budj Bim Cultural Landscape is a UNESCO World Heritage site.

MAIN: TYSON LOVETT-MURRAY, GUNDITJ MIRRING TRADITIONAL OWNERS ABORIGINAL CORPORATION

INSET: DENISBIN/FLICKR.COM/CC BY-ND 2.0

GROWING KNOWLEDGE OVER GENERATIONS

The Meriam children's knowledge of seafood and ocean environments has come from their parents, families, friends and cultural practices, or ways of life. This kind of learning—observing and passing knowledge down over many generations—doesn't just happen in the Torres Strait Islands. Along many of the world's coastlines there are Indigenous Peoples whose families have been living in the same place and using resources from the sea for hundreds or thousands of years. First Nations and Inuit in Canada, Native Americans in the United States, Kānaka Maoli in the Hawaiian Islands, Māori in Aotearoa New Zealand, Quechua in Peru, Maya in Mexico and Guatemala, Yaghan in Tierra del Fuego and Ainu in Japan are just a few Peoples who have lived with the oceans for eons.

Archaeologists have recorded tens of thousands of wooden stakes in a fish-trap complex in Comox Harbour on Vancouver Island.
NANCY GREENE

MANY TYPES OF SCIENCE, MANY TYPES OF KNOWLEDGE

If we live in one place near the sea for a long time and watch our surroundings day to day, we make observations about how ocean animals, plants, currents, waves, weather patterns, rocks and sand are all interconnected and rely on one another. Scientists do this, too, by using scientific methods and experiments over shorter periods of time. Today Western scientists (scientists trained in the *scientific method*) are realizing that there are additional types of science and ways of understanding the world around us. They are recognizing the importance and longevity of Traditional Knowledge found in Indigenous communities. Scientific information doesn't always have to appear as numbers and data. It can be passed from generation to generation in language, stories, songs and cultural practices. Some of these ancient practices can help restore the health of our oceans today.

Field Notes

My friend Q̓íx̌itasu Yím̓ázalas, Elroy White, is the owner of Central Coast Archaeology in Bella Bella, BC. As a **Haíɫzaqv** archaeologist, Elroy's experiences at archaeological sites are different than mine. We both look for the evidence people have left behind, and we both use the scientific methods we've learned through archaeology. But when Elroy visits places in his territory, he also hears the songs and stories that have been passed down through generations. He thinks about the dances and family trees that are connected to those places. He remembers the generations of family before him and considers the generations after him that will continue to live throughout Haíɫzaqv territory. He is guided by his potlatching traditions and laws. He is connected to the places he visits in much deeper and more personal ways than I will ever know. Thank you, Elroy, for allowing me to share this.

COURTESY OF ELROY WHITE

HAWAIIAN FISHPONDS

The Kānaka Maoli in the Hawaiian Islands have been farming fish for over 1,500 years. Their loko kuapā (walled fishponds built near the shoreline) are still used today to care for fish and other seafood. The pond walls enclose a section of shoreline ranging in length from 50 yards (45.7 meters) to over a mile (1.6 kilometers) and reaching a height of as much as 6 feet (1.8 meters) or more. Many people must work together to build these walls and care for the ponds. There is a role for everyone, young and old, as rocks of different sizes are added to the walls. People build special gates to allow small fish into the pond from the open ocean. The ponds' waters are full of tasty phytoplankton and algae that attract the baby fish. Eventually the fish grow too big to leave and remain in the pond until people are ready to catch them.

A great way to photograph loko kuapā is from the sky. This is the He'eia Fishpond in Oahu, HI.
PAEPAE O HE'EIA

Caring for loko kuapā and loko i'a kalo requires teamwork. Gates allow small fish to enter but stop the big fish from leaving.
MAIN: JAMIE MAKASOBE
INSET: KIMBERLY MOA

CONNECTING LAND AND SEA

The loko kuapā are connected to streams or underground springs inland. Most coastal ponds have brackish (salty and fresh) water, while fishponds inland are filled entirely with fresh water. Different kinds of fish and prawns grow in these ponds. The loko i'a kalo (inland ponds) also grow taro. Taro is an important vegetable with edible roots and leaves. Fishponds are found throughout valleys and are part of food systems that span many miles from mountaintop to seafloor. The Kānaka Maoli understand that they must not just take from these places but give back too. In addition to fishing, people adjust water levels inland, remove predators and repair walls. By caring for the ponds throughout the year, the people make sure each fishpond can adjust to changes in the environment. This traditional practice recognizes that land and ocean ecosystems are connected, and is a sustainable way to produce food.

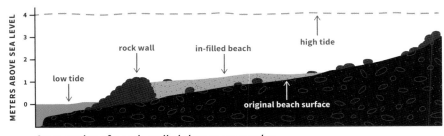

Cross section of a rock-walled clam or sea garden.

ADAPTED FROM DIAGRAM ORIGINALLY CREATED BY DANA LEPOFSKY, HAUYAT.CA

(Top) This clam garden is more than 3,000 years old! (Bottom) A crab, sea cucumber and whelk snuggle up against the boulders in a sea-garden wall.

NICOLE SMITH

SEA GARDENS OF THE PACIFIC NORTHWEST

For thousands of years, Indigenous Peoples along the northwest coast of North America have been building rock walls to care for marine species too. The rock walls built at the lowest tide protect beaches and create habitat for sea creatures like clams. They are home to many other traditional foods too—crabs, sea cucumbers, whelks, sea urchins, chitons, barnacles, kelps and octopi, to name a few. These walled beaches are known as clam gardens or sea gardens in English. Wherever there is a rock wall at the low-tide level, sand, pebbles and broken shells build up behind the wall and flatten the beach, creating a calmer place for the baby clams to grow. There are often more clams in sea gardens than in natural beaches, and they grow faster too. When Indigenous people dig clams, they care for the gardens by turning over the sediments, clearing away seaweed and logs, and returning rocks to the wall so the beaches will stay healthy.

RESTORING BEACHES FOR FUTURE GENERATIONS

In the past, hundreds of sea gardens would have been in use up and down the Pacific Northwest coast. But when Europeans arrived in North America, they introduced diseases and colonial practices that separated Indigenous people from their families, lands, beaches and waters. As a result, many sea gardens along the Pacific coast were no longer used. Today Elders talk about how the beaches aren't as healthy as they once were. Scientists studying clam gardens are also finding that clams were healthier in the past.

This group is hard at work caring for beaches and adding rocks to the wall of a sea garden in the Gulf Islands.
NICOLE SMITH

Fortunately many First Nations and Native American communities along the northwest coast are restoring and using sea gardens again. In the southern Gulf Islands, the Hul'q'umi'num' and W̱SÁNEĆ Nations are working with Elders, youth, scientists, teachers and volunteers, and Parks Canada to restore the beaches. They are all learning from Indigenous knowledge holders how to care for these places in traditional ways once again. This includes making the rock walls higher so the gardens work with today's rising sea levels.

Traditional Knowledge that has grown in a place over generations can offer solutions for oceans today. It teaches us that people are connected to the ocean and not separate from it. If we want to live on a healthy planet, we must treat the plants, animals, rivers, oceans, mountains and ecosystems around us respectfully. We must actively care for our beaches, valleys and water sources every time we visit them. When we do this, we make our beaches healthier for today and into the future.

Arti-fact

There are more than two dozen Indigenous languages along the Pacific Northwest coast of North America. Some words for clam garden or sea garden are lúx̱ʷxiwey in Kwak'wala, t'iimiik̓ in Nuu-chah-nulth, or wúx̱ʷuthin in éy7á7juuthem, a Coast Salish language.

CHAPTER FOUR

Archaeology of the Future

GARBOLOGY

Have you ever looked in your neighbor's recycling or garbage bin while walking to school? If so, could you tell how many people lived in the home? Were they old? Young like you? Did they order pizza recently? Perhaps you noticed changes in their recycling throughout the year, especially over the holidays. If you've done this or asked any of these questions, you were being an archaeologist! You were figuring out how people lived based on what they left behind. But did you stop and wonder about how much of their garbage will survive into the future? I often think about what we're leaving for people to find hundreds and thousands of years from now. What stories will their discoveries tell about us?

Every two weeks blue bins full of recyclable paper, plastic and glass line the streets of our neighborhood.
NICOLE SMITH

Arti-fact

Some archaeologists today examine people's garbage. This field of study is known as *garbology*.

RETURNING TO THE EARTH

Today we find only a few things that people used in the past. That's because our ancestors mostly used natural materials that disappear over time. Along the northwest coast of North America, where I do most of my work, more than 95 percent of the objects people made in the distant past have decomposed. Some of the thousand-year-old houses constructed of cedar have fallen down and are covered in moss and ferns or have become *nursing trees*. Most house posts and beams have decomposed entirely and returned to the soil. The Indigenous ancestors along this coastline made good use of natural materials, and most of their tools and material items from thousands of years ago have become part of nature once again.

Arti-fact

Special items are often passed from generation to generation. These *heirlooms* can be hundreds of years old, and they remind us of who we are and of our history. Do you have any heirlooms in your home?

A traditional house post and beam being reclaimed by the forest.
NICOLE SMITH

The interior of a house at the Neolithic village of Skara Brae in the Orkney Islands, Scotland.
ELEANOR SCRIVEN/ROBERTHARDING/GETTY IMAGES

INSTEAD OF WOOD

The same story can be told in many other places in the world. If people didn't have immense forests and wood available to build their homes, they would use other natural materials like stone or bone. At Skara Brae, in the Orkney Islands in the north of Scotland, there is barely a tree to be seen. That would have been the case 5,000 years ago. At that time, the early farmers found ways of constructing their homes and villages out of stone slabs. Even their sleeping areas, dressers and chairs were made of stone. Aside from the different materials used in housing, many of the artifacts preserved at Skara Brae look similar to ones we find on the northwest coast of North America. In both places, stone, bone and shell tools have been flaked, whittled or ground down to create knives, points, awls, axes, chisels, bowls, game pieces, jewelry and other artifacts whose function we will likely never understand. Everything else they might have used has decomposed and returned to soil.

THE GROUND IS THAWING

In most archaeological sites, people's household objects have decomposed because they were *organic*. Very occasionally, however, archaeologists find a site where organic materials have been preserved. These sites are usually found in extremely dry, waterlogged or frozen places. Where the Mackenzie River meets the Arctic Ocean, archaeologists have been recovering parts of the Inuvialuit village of Kuukpak. The Inuvialuit lived in this village for several centuries, right up until the mid- to late 1800s. The nearby river estuary was an important place to hunt beluga whales in the summer.

Recently an archaeological team has been trying to save a 500-year-old home at Kuukpak before it washes into the sea. The house was semi-subterranean—meaning it was built into the ground. Driftwood was used for the roof, walls and floor, and the whole house was covered with sod—large mats of grass and soil. This type of architecture would have protected the people from the cold Arctic weather. For hundreds of years this house survived mostly intact because the ground around it was frozen. But today, because of climate change, the permafrost is thawing, and the house and everything inside it are at risk of rotting.

Sea-level rise and bigger storms are causing the shoreline to move inland by as much as a yard (almost a meter) each year. The Inuvialuit home and archaeological site could be washed into the ocean within a few short years. Archaeologists are racing to recover as much information as they can. Near a bench along the back wall, they found a collection of personal items including a comb, knife and intact fishhook. These are precious items from a time when people had much less stuff than we do today.

Beluga ribs lying on the beach near the Inuvialuit village of Kuukpak.
MAX FRIESEN

A boy from a nomadic family in Kyrgyzstan stands in front of his yurt.
THE ROAD PROVIDES/SHUTTERSTOCK.COM

WHAT DO YOUR BELONGINGS SAY ABOUT YOU?

The number of personal items in a home depends on the family's lifestyle. As in the past, people today live in many different ways. Some of us are city dwellers and others live in the country. Some people farm or garden, some go to the grocery store, and some of us collect, hunt and fish for our foods. Some of us are nomadic, meaning that we travel from one place to another, moving our homes throughout the year on the backs of animals like camels, reindeer or yaks. The number of belongings we surround ourselves with depends on our day-to-day activities and our beliefs about the world around us.

If you scan your own home, how many items do you see? What stories do they tell about you? Perhaps they show that you like sports, art or music. Maybe they reveal that you have a large family or live with animals. Your belongings reflect what you, your family and community think are important. What they are made of can also tell stories about our beliefs. As you look around your home, you may have spotted a material type that is very new on this planet—plastic! What does plastic say about our relationships with the world?

How many different materials are used to make a guitar?
JORDI SALAS/GETTY IMAGES

BONKERS FOR BILLIARD BALLS

Plastic was invented in 1868—less than 200 years ago. Around that time, billiards was a popular game in North America and Europe. Billiard balls are about the size of tennis balls and were initially made of ivory from elephant tusks. As billiards became more common, people grew concerned about how many majestic animals were being killed just so people could play a game. Celluloid was the first plastic invented to replace ivory.

By the early 1900s additional **synthetic** plastics were being created, replacing natural materials like wood, plants, metal, stone and bone in the manufacturing of many kinds of goods. Plastic was cheaper than natural materials, allowing people to buy more things for their homes than ever before. Even though plastic was invented to save the natural world, it could also be thrown away very easily. As we now know, a big problem with plastic is that it doesn't decompose. By the 1960s people had started worrying about how much plastic was appearing in the oceans.

A billiard ball from 1868, one of the first to be made of celluloid.
DIVISION OF MEDICINE AND SCIENCE, NATIONAL MUSEUM OF AMERICAN HISTORY, SMITHSONIAN INSTITUTION

Main: A mountain of plastic at a recycling plant. Do we really need all the plastic items we buy?

Inset: Plastic breaks down into smaller and smaller pieces over time, eventually becoming tiny particles called microplastics.

MAIN: RON LEVINE/GETTY IMAGES;

INSET: NAVAPAN ASSAVASUNTAKUL/SHUTTERSTOCK.COM

Using cloth bags for shopping is a great way to reduce plastic.

MARCIA FERNANDES/GETTY IMAGES

THE PLASTIC AGE?

Today plastic is everywhere. It's in the sea, soil, glaciers and sometimes in the food we eat and the water we drink. Having plastic everywhere affects our health and the health of the planet. When archaeologists look back, we often classify periods of time based on the most common material types we find. This is why we use terms like Stone Age, Bronze Age and Iron Age. What will archaeologists call the 1900s and early 2000s? Will our time be the Plastic Age? And what does all this plastic say about our beliefs, what we value and our relationships with nature and the ocean?

REDUCE, REUSE, RECYCLE

My hope is that we can bring the Plastic Age to a quick end or at least use less of this material from day to day. Kids around the world are working to reduce their use of plastic. Many students are bringing reusable lunch kits and water bottles to school instead of prepacked foods and drink boxes with plastic straws that can be thrown away. My daughter and her friends have sewn reusable cloth bags to use as gift wrap and goodie bags at birthdays. And instead of giving plastic toys as presents, some young people are giving gift certificates for things like a visit to a trampoline park or a trip to the movie theater. Experiences like these don't create much waste.

An underwater archaeologist excavates a clam garden.
PARKS CANADA UNDERWATER ARCHAEOLOGY TEAM

Field Notes

A few years ago I had an opportunity to work with the Parks Canada Underwater Archaeology Team to excavate clam gardens in the Salish Sea. We learned that the Coast Salish Peoples have been using clam gardens for at least 4,000 years! The biggest difference I noticed between underwater and land-based archaeology was that things move more slowly in water because the underwater archaeologists have to plan every move very carefully before they dive. They have to wear scuba gear and use hand signals and wireless systems to communicate. They take notes, collect samples, draw maps and adjust their suction excavation machine while wearing thick gloves, and they carry weights so they don't float away. I imagine this is what archaeology would be like on the moon.

SMALL STEPS, BIG CHANGE

Kids can help adults change their plastic habits too. Here are a few simple ways to get started:

- Buy milk in paper cartons or glass bottles.
- Use strips of dried laundry detergent.
- Use cloth bags when shopping.
- Drink through metal straws.
- Bake cookies and treats instead of buying packaged ones.
- Use reusable water bottles.
- Buy concentrated juices and add water at home.
- Wash hair with a shampoo soap bar.
- Grow, fish and collect your own food.

Can you think of ways to reduce your use of plastic?
SOLSTOCK/GETTY IMAGES

THE FUTURE

Certainly plastic has many important uses, and its use for specialized items like medical and computer equipment will probably continue for some time. But do we need all the other items? People have managed to live without plastic for most of human history. I admire our ancestors' lifestyles and how environmentally friendly they were. And since there is only so much we can understand from looking at people's artifacts and features, I am glad that traditional wisdom survives in Indigenous communities for us to learn from today. By bringing together these many forms of knowledge from past and present, I feel hopeful that we can improve the health of our oceans and planet in the future. It might mean leaving less behind for future archaeologists to find, but that's okay. Archaeologists love a good mystery.

We all thrive when our oceans are plastic-free.
CHARLES BROUGHER/GETTY IMAGES

Have you ever spotted something on land and wondered how it got there?
STEFAN CRISTIAN CIOATA/GETTY IMAGES

Acknowledgments

There are many people to acknowledge for supporting this book. I am grateful to Ann Eriksson and Kay Weisman for the initial nudges; Kirstie Hudson, Georgia Bradburne, Dahlia Yuen, and the Orca team for fantastic support, editorial suggestions and guidance; and to colleagues and friends from North America who gave permissions, comments, moral support and/or advice on content: Skye Augustine, Rebecca Bliege Bird, Jenny Cohen, Camille Collinson, Daryl Fedje, Max Friesen, Nancy Greene, Gwaii Haanas National Park Reserve and Haida Heritage Site, Hakai Institute, Huu-ay-aht First Nations, Jude Isabella, Kat Johnnie, Rita Johnson, Erich Kelch, Dana Lepofsky, Quentin Mackie, Al Mackie, Glen MacKay, Alan McMillan, Iain and Flora McKechnie, Jon Moore, Caron Olive, Parks Canada, Eric Pelkey, Stella Peters, Christine Roberts, Darrell Ross, Darlene Small, Denis St. Claire, Gemma Tarling, Tseshaht First Nation, Wahmeesh Ken Watts, Elroy White, Barbara Wilson, and Louie Wilson. To those oceans away, thank you for your time and thoughtful comments to help me understand aspects of your beautiful cultures and for tolerating Zoom calls, emails and/or visits from Canada: Brenda Asuncion, Trakka Clarke, Gunditj Mirring Traditional Owners Aboriginal Corporation RNTBC, Maria Paz Martinoli, Angelica Tivoli, Lucy Wailu and Francisco Zangrando. Where possible, I have reached out directly to communities and researchers for permissions to share aspects of their heritage or research. When distance, language barriers or timing made this tricky, I have relied on published works or well publicized examples. Any errors are my own.

To my Indigenous colleagues and friends who have trusted me to share a piece of your cultural heritage, thank you. I am grateful for the knowledge you have shared, which helps us understand the importance of archaeological and cultural heritage to people today, from the past and those still coming. I hope this book honors you and your ancestors' legacies.

Thank you to my parents for their love, editorial guidance and hard work to instill in me from an early age an appreciation of books and writing.

Resources

Print

Buhrman-Deever, Susannah. Illus. Matthew Trueman. *If You Take Away the Otter.* Candlewick Press, 2020.

Eriksson, Ann. *Dive In! Exploring Our Connection with the Ocean.* Orca Book Publishers, 2018.

Moloney, Norah. *The Young Oxford Book of Archaeology.* Oxford University Press, 1997.

Mulder, Michelle. *Trash Talk: Moving Toward a Zero-Waste World.* Orca Book Publishers, 2015.

Weisman, Kay. Illus. Roy Henry Vickers. *If You Want to Visit a Sea Garden.* Groundwood Books, 2020.

Online

American Museum of Natural History: amnh.org/explore/ology/archaeology

BC Archives: search-bcarchives.royalbcmuseum.bc.ca

Hakai Magazine, "Videos and Visuals" (*search for archaeology***):** hakaimagazine.com/videos-visuals

Húýat: hauyat.ca/index.html

Kids Discover Archaeology: online.kidsdiscover.com/unit/archaeology

National Park Service, "Archeology for Kids": nps.gov/subjects/archeology/archeology-for-kids.htm

Pacific Herring: Past, Present and Future: pacificherring.org

Sea Gardens Across the Pacific: seagardens.net

Sealaska Heritage: sealaskaheritage.org

Glossary

aquaculture—cultivation of water (aquatic) species for food, including freshwater and saltwater species

archaeological site—any place that has evidence of people who lived there in the past; usually more than 50 years old

archaeologist—a person who studies the human past by examining the things that people have left behind

archaeology—the study of how people lived in the past

artifact—an item, made or modified by people, that can be picked up and moved

diatoms—single-celled algae that live in salty, fresh and brackish water and have skeletons made of silica

direct evidence—evidence that links directly to the event or fact in question. For example, a boat is direct evidence of travel over water.

feature—something made by people that cannot be picked up without being taken apart

geoduck—a very large saltwater clam found on the West Coast of North America that digs very deep and has a giant neck

glaciation—refers to the creation, movement and melting of glaciers. Often used to refer to the time in the past when glaciers covered much of the world's land. Also known as an *ice age.*

Haíłzaqv—people from the Heiltsuk Nation

heirlooms—special objects passed down from one generation to the next

hominin—an early human or early species very closely related to humans. Includes Neanderthals, our closest human relative, who first appeared in Europe around 400,000 years ago.

indirect evidence—evidence that suggests something occurred but doesn't prove it directly. For example, albatross bones in an archaeological site suggest that people caught albatross. Since albatross live far offshore, the bones provide indirect evidence that people had boats to be able to catch the birds.

Industrial Revolution—the time in history when humans started to use machines to create goods and materials, beginning in the mid-1700s

jigging—fishing in salt or fresh water with a lure that causes the line to move up and down in a jerking motion

millennia—thousands of years

nursing trees—fallen trees that give protection and nutrients to younger trees, helping them grow. Young trees often grow on top of nursing trees.

organic—material that is or was once living

scientific method—the procedure scientists use to understand phenomena in our world. When a scientist observes something in the natural world, they will then make a prediction or hypothesis about what they see. They test their hypothesis to determine if it is true or not. The test may require experiments. The experiments will generate information that needs to be analyzed. The results of the tests or experiments shape the scientist's understanding of the world.

sediment—small pieces of rock or mineral, like sand and silt, that can be moved by wind or water

synthetic—something that does not occur naturally and is made by a chemical process

Index

SAMANTHA BIROSH

NICOLE F. SMITH is an archaeologist, educator and speaker. Since 2000, archaeological research has taken her throughout coastal British Columbia, to the Northwest Territories and to Tierra del Fuego in southernmost Argentina. She has worked with over 20 First Nations communities throughout BC and academic colleagues to broaden the knowledge about coastal heritage, focusing on clam gardens, fish traps, stone tools, archaeological sites over 10,000 years old and the effects of climate change and sea-level rise on cultural heritage. Her teams' results have been published internationally and recognized in the media, including the BBC, CBC's *Quirks & Quarks* and *Hakai Magazine*. She loves working with grade-school students to help them learn more about archaeology. Nicole lives with her family on the Traditional Territories of the Coast Salish Peoples on southern Vancouver Island, British Columbia. *Dig Deep* is her first book.